19 February 2017

Mr. John Berry, P.C., L.L.O.
Berry Law Firm
2650 North 48th Street
Lincoln, NE 68504

Dear John,

Thank you so much for sending two copies of your new book "The Next Battle." I kept one copy and the other I provided to my associate in Senator Fischer's Omaha office. Both of us work veterans' issues; there is that much to do to assist them.

Your book is unique in that it communicates using common words and terms. So many guides for veterans use time worn bureaucratic language difficult to understand and make reference to obscure and difficult to understand regulations. When veterans seek help from Senator Fischer we often find they are overwhelmed by complexity when the key issues of their claims are actually simple.

Keep up the good work helping Nebraska's military veterans.

Sincerely,

Roger P. Lempke
Lt. Gen. (Nebr. Ret.)

"The Berry Law Firm is a godsend. After a seemingly never-ending battle with the VA to get the benefits that I need to live a normal life, I had almost given up hope.

A friend of mine told me about this wonderful team of lawyers and I figured I didn't have anything to lose. I gave them a call and in less than 6 months I went from living in a shelter for veterans with health problems to living in my own home and having the ability to pay for my everyday needs.

If there is anyone who has any doubt about this awesome team just take it from me – they did in 6 months what I couldn't do in more than 6 years."

Miles B.
South Carolina

"I started at 20 percent and now I'm at 100. They kept appealing and coming up with new ammunition. They don't quit, they keep going. It's been a godsend for us."

Gary M.
Washington

The Next Battle

A Guide to Veterans Disability Benefits

email: intake@ptsdlawyers.com
phone: 888.883.2483

The Next Battle

A Guide to Veterans Disability Benefits

John S. Berry

Check us out online at ptsdlawyers.com
Call us at 888.883.2483

Published by:
Sabrequill Press
Lincoln, Nebraska

Printed in the United States of America
ISBN: 978-0998264004

Contact the Author at:
Sabrequill Press
2650 North 48th Street
Lincoln, NE 68504
www.ptsdlawyers.com
1.888.883.2483

Images by vecteezy.com

Contents

Why We Help Veterans

The Berry Law Firm was established in 1965 by my father, John Stevens Berry Sr., who served three tours in Vietnam. Berry Sr. branch-transferred from Infantry to JAG and was chief defense counsel for Vietnam's largest general court martial jurisdiction. He travelled the length and breadth of Vietnam, protecting the rights of GIs. His book, *Those Gallant Men*, details his successful legal defense of members of the 5th Special Forces in Vietnam charged with murdering a double agent. After Vietnam, Berry Sr. practiced civil litigation and criminal defense. Berry Sr. often assisted fellow Vietnam veterans with legal problems associated with what is now known as PTSD. He would go on to represent numerous veterans pro bono in their struggles with VA regional offices and the Court of Veterans Appeals.

Berry Sr.'s uncle and first law partner, Wade Stevens, was a pilot during WWI. The Stevens and Berry families served overseas in WWII and Korea. John Stevens was wounded twice at Vicksburg while serving with the 9th Iowa Infantry during the Civil War.

I led a mechanized infantry platoon in Bosnia/Kosavo, and commanded a company in Iraq. I am currently a lieutenant colonel in the Nebraska National Guard.

We are honored to represent veterans in need of legal assistance. Lawyers talk a lot about constitutional rights. We help veterans who sacrificed to protect those rights.

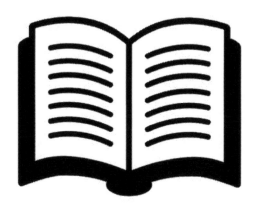

Why You Should Read This Book

The purpose of this book is to provide veterans with an understanding of the Department of Veterans' Affairs (VA) appeals process and provide advocacy tips for successful VA appeals. Jim's story below demonstrates why veterans should read this book.

Jim served with the 1st Cavalry Division in Vietnam. He was injured several times during his military service but avoided medics and sick call as much as he could. When Jim came home he was immediately discharged, so he moved on with his life. When Jim's injuries didn't heal, he sought assistance from the VA. Jim's experience there was horrific. Veterans' Administration officials told him he was wasting their time. Feeling ashamed, Jim remembered that he served with a lot of great soldiers who had far worse injuries than his and decided not to file a disability claim and to never return to the VA.

Fifteen years later, at a Vietnam Veterans Reunion, Jim ran into his old squad leader who told him to pursue VA benefits.

After years of regularly attending these reunions, Jim finally filed claims at his VA regional office. Within a year, Jim received service connection for hearing loss and tinnitus but his claims for post-traumatic stress disorder (PTSD), lower back pain and a right knee injury were denied. Jim appealed the decision to the Board of Veterans Appeals (BVA) where once again his conditions were denied.

Jim felt discouraged, but every year at the Vietnam Veterans Reunion, fellow veterans encouraged him to fight the VA and continue the appeals process. Because he respected the opinions of other combat veterans, Jim continued to appeal.

At a later Vietnam Veterans Reunion, Jim met an attorney who offered to help him appeal his case to the Court of Appeals for Veterans Claims (CAVC), a court that makes decisions independent of the VA. Jim's attorney won the case and Jim was directed to go back to the VA for another Compensation and Pension (C&P) examination. Soon after the exam, the VA granted Jim service connection for his lower back and right knee conditions, but continued to deny his claims for PTSD. After ten more years of fighting, the VA awarded Jim service connection for PTSD, too.

Jim's story is not unique. Veterans who appeal cases rarely win the disability compensation they deserve on the first appeal. The common cycle is appeal, remand, denial, appeal, remand, denial. Veterans caught in this cycle often become discouraged and abandon their clams. This is unfortunate because once a veteran abandons his or her claim, not only is the effective date of the claim lost, but he or she must submit "new and material evidence" to reopen the claim.

The most common complaints we hear from veterans concern the amount of time it takes the VA to adjudicate a claim. The biggest problem is not that the VA is taking a long time to adjudicate claims (although the VA does take a ridiculously long time to adjudicate claims), but instead that if a veteran does not win the appeal the first time around, he or she will have to start over in the VA appeals process. Once again, the cycle of appeal, remand, denial sucks years away from a veterans' disability compensation payments and often discourages veterans from pursuing future appeals.

If you get one sliver of wisdom from this book it should be this: You earned your VA benefits, but you may have to fight for them. The VA appeals system is set up so that if you become discouraged and do not appeal, it will be more difficult for you to win your disability claims in the future.

While serving your country, you never quit. You didn't quit when the Drill Sergeant yelled at you, you didn't quit when you were injured, you didn't quit during training, you didn't quit during deployment, and you didn't quit during wars. You sacrificed to earn the honor of being a veteran. In your fight to get your VA benefits, your best weapons are knowledge and persistence. Do not let the VA discourage you from obtaining the disability benefits you earned.

Introduction

This book discusses winning strategies in the battle for service-connected VA disability compensation. The battle is broken down into three fights:

1. Service connection is the first and most critical fight. If a veteran cannot convince the VA that his or her disability was caused by or occurred in military service, the battle is lost.

2. The next fight is obtaining the correct disability rating. Veterans often feel cheated by the VA when they receive a disability rating lower than what they expected. Disability ratings are important because they determine the monthly amount of disability compensation a veteran receives from the VA.

3. The final fight is for the correct effective date. The effective date is the day when veterans are supposed to begin receiving disability compensation. When the VA gets the effective date wrong, a disabled veteran could lose thousands of dollars in disability compensation.

The stories in this book are based on fact patterns the Berry Law Firm routinely encounters when assisting veterans with their VA appeals.

Chapter One
Getting Service-Connected

It all starts with service connection, the VA's acknowledgment of the link between a current disability and past military service. In order for a veteran to get disability compensation for an injury or disease, the following must be established:

1. A current disability or disease;

2. Adequate evidence showing that the cause of the disability or disease occurred in-service or resulted from an in-service event or that a disability or disease was aggravated in-service; and

3. Competent evidence of a link or nexus between an in-service injury or aggravation and a current disability or disease.

Service connection does not just apply to events that occurred during duty hours. As the drill sergeants said: "The military owns you 24/7." Disabilities caused by events that occurred off-duty are usually considered to have happened in the line of duty unless the injury resulted from the veteran's willful misconduct.

Simply put, if a veteran served on active federal service at the time of the injury, he or she will probably meet the active service requirement for service connection.

In the National Guard and Reserves it can be more difficult to prove that an injury occurred in the line of duty. If the injury occurred during IDT, drill, or battle assembly (or whatever the unit calls their weekend obligation), it's probably covered. Unfortunately, when National Guard members are injured on state orders rather than federal orders, the VA will not service-connect. Service connection requires active federal service.

Mike's story illustrates how an off-duty injury can be service-connected.

When Mike deployed to Iraq he decided to save his money so he could buy a Harley-Davidson Wide Glide motorcycle upon his return. At the time, Harley Davison offered good deals to deployed soldiers. By saving his hostile pay and family separation pay, Mike was able to buy the Harley within a month of returning home.

On base, Mike took a motorcycle safety class and made sure to wear all the required protective gear while riding. One Saturday afternoon, Mike decided to take a five-hour trip to visit one of his buddies in North Carolina. Ten miles from his friend's residence, a car switching lanes on the highway forced Mike off the road and into a ditch at 50 mph. The Wide Glide was totaled and Mike suffered injuries to his C5 and C6 vertebrae.

After a couple of weeks in the hospital and long months of rehabilitation, Mike returned to his unit and completed his enlistment. When Mike initially filed for disability, the VA denied his claim and stated that his injury did not occur in the line of duty and that even if it did, his negligence on the motorcycle constituted willful misconduct. After years of fighting the VA, Mike won on appeal because he was injured while on active federal service and the accident was not caused by willful misconduct.

Requirement #1:
Evidence of a Current Disability

An in-service injury does not always result in a current disability. Most service members sustain some type of in-service injury that may be temporary in nature. A paratrooper who blows out a knee during a rough landing at Frye Drop Zone is not entitled to service connection for his injury unless the knee is currently disabled when he applies for disability benefits.

In the army, an injured soldier may obtain a temporary profile which exempts him or her from performing activities that could aggravate an injury. Once the injury heals, the temporary profile expires and the soldier's activities are no longer medically restricted. If a veteran is still suffering from that injury after being discharged, the veteran has a current disability for VA purposes.

The VA often fails to provide disabled veterans with accurate diagnoses. Some veterans injured in-service need to go outside of the VA to get an opinion from a doctor stating that they have a current disability.

For example, an Army Specialist named Jamie had a sore ankle after a 12-mile road march. Two days later she injured the same ankle during a run. About a week later, when the injury became unbearable, Jamie went to sick call and discovered she had a stress fracture. The unit doc put Jamie on profile. Eventually the stress fracture healed and within a couple of months Jamie was able to continue to run and ruck-march. After her discharge, Jamie continued to live an active lifestyle and ran several 10k races and half marathons. Jamie's ankle never felt the same after the stress fracture but she was able to deal with the pain.

Years later, the pain prevented Jamie from running. When Jamie applied for VA disability benefits, the VA determined that she did not have a current disability and denied that the in-service stress fracture was causing what her private doctor diagnosed as several different conditions. The VA determined that pain alone was not sufficient for service connection.

What Is a Current Disability?

Jamie's ankle condition was insufficient for VA service connection because her claims file (C-file) lacked medical evidence of a current disability. The medical evidence the VA requires can be a specific diagnosis or statements based on accepted medical principles acknowledging a current disability. The diagnoses must be made by a medical professional or someone with specialized knowledge or training.

In Jamie's case, while her in-service injury and pain did not constitute a diagnosis, it did trigger the VA to provide her with a medical examination. In hindsight, if Jamie provided the VA with medical records from her private doctor at the time she filed her claim, she probably would have been service-connected sooner.

In one instance, Berry Law Firm represented a veteran who worked as a registered nurse. The veteran provided a statement in which he diagnosed his own condition. The VA initially found the veteran's statement was not competent evidence because it was a lay statement from the veteran diagnosing his own condition. However, after Berry Law Firm reminded the VA that the veteran was a registered nurse, the VA found the self-diagnoses to be competent medical evidence of a current diagnosis.

If a veteran cannot obtain a medical examination from the VA or the VA doctor finds that the veteran does not have a current disability, the veteran has the right to submit a separate medical opinion from a private doctor.

When VA Medical Staff Claim a Veteran Doesn't Have a Disability

Many veterans who jump through hoops to obtain a medical examination from the VA are disappointed when VA medical personnel find the veteran does not have a diagnosed injury. Note - I did not say "VA doctor." In many instances, C&P examinations are not performed by medical doctors but rather by physician assistants or nurse practitioners.

When a veteran has multiple medical opinions in his C-file that contradict one another, the VA will weigh the credibility and value of each opinion. If the VA finds the weight of the negative opinions greater than the weight of the opinions supporting the diagnosis, the VA will deny the claim. However, if the evidence is balanced, the VA must find that there is a current disability because the presumption goes to the veteran's benefit.

It is not unusual for a VA doctor to disagree with a veteran's private physician. One highly successful tactic Berry Law Firm uses is to send the VA the private doctor's resume (commonly known as a Curriculum Vitae) to argue that the private doctor's opinion should carry more weight because he or she is a specialist or is more experienced or accomplished than the VA's doctor.

Occasionally, the VA will use a physician assistant or nurse to provide an opinion. In these instances, when a veteran has a private doctor's opinion confirming a diagnosis, the VA will generally choose the M.D.'s confirmed diagnosis over the opinion of any non-doctor medical professionals who contradict the medical opinion – but not always.

Additionally, a private doctor's diagnosis is more persuasive when supported by a discussion of specific facts from the veteran's service records or medical history. In many instances when a private physician states he reviewed a veteran's claims file and specifically cites medical records or in-service events, the veteran stands a better chance of getting service-connected.

Requirement #2:
Proving an In-Service Injury

Once the VA acknowledges that a veteran has a current disability, the VA will consider whether the veteran's injury or disease was caused or aggravated by military service. This is often referred to as an "in-service injury" for physical injuries or an "in-service stressor" for mental health conditions.

In reality, when most veterans were injured in service they did not immediately seek medical treatment. Many service members hide injuries during military service for fear that they will be placed on a profile and become ineligible for favorable personnel actions or assignments. A service member's willingness to fight through the pain can make it difficult for him or her to obtain disability compensation after discharge. A veteran who failed to disclose an injury during service faces the difficult burden of establishing that the disability was caused in-service. However, a lack of service medical records or other documentation of injury does not mean the veteran cannot establish the injury occurred in-service.

Buddy Statements: Getting by with a Little Help from Your Friends

Veterans often submit "buddy statements" (or lay statements) from fellow service members who witnessed the veteran's injury and can corroborate the time, location, date and circumstances surrounding the injury. These buddy statements can be important even if in-service documentation of the injury exists.

For example, while serving in a mortar platoon humping mortar tubes through the jungles of Vietnam, Steve fell down a steep hill and seriously injured his back. Steve received medical treatment for his back, but the records never reached his C-File. Fortunately, Steve stayed in contact with several members of his platoon who were able to provide statements corroborating his back injury. Steve's platoon members saw him fall down the hill, helped him retrieve his gear, and observed how the back injury affected Steve throughout the rest of his tour in Vietnam.

Unfortunately, many veterans do not keep in touch with former unit members who witnessed their injuries. Even if there is some evidence in the veteran's service medical records showing he or she incurred an injury in-service, the medical opinion provided by the VA may still deny that the in-service injury caused the current disability.

In these circumstances, the veteran has the option of obtaining an independent examination of his or her service medical records by a private physician who may provide a written opinion as to whether there was an event or injury in-service that caused his or her current disability.

In some instances, the VA isn't convinced by a private doctor's opinion or a veteran's statements about his or her own injuries. For this reason, corroboration through buddy statements, photographs, and even letters home may be crucial in establishing that a veteran incurred a disability in-service.

In Steve's case, not only did the buddy statements from members of his platoon corroborate Steve's in-service event that caused his back injury, they also explained how the event affected Steve's ability to carry gear and do his job throughout his tour in Vietnam.

Broken, Aggravated, and Presumed Sound

Proud veterans know that not everyone is fit to serve. The military only accepts those of sound mind and body. So if a service member is "broken" when discharged, the military is responsible.

All branches of the military conduct medical entrance examinations of potential service members and determine whether they are fit to serve. Once a Solider, Marine, Sailor, or Airman is accepted into the military and placed on active duty there is a presumption that the service member is physically and mentally sound. Therefore, if a veteran develops a disability in-service or shortly thereafter, the VA presumes this injury or disability was caused by active military service.

Additionally, if the veteran had any medical conditions noted on his or her entrance examination, the veteran may argue the previously existing health issues were aggravated by military service and subject to VA compensation. Even though the veteran may have been a little "broken" upon entry into service, if the injury or disability gets worse in-service, the veteran may receive compensation for the military's role in aggravating his or her injury or disability.

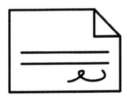

Credible Combat Veteran Statements

Combat veterans have an advantage in that their statements regarding events that occurred during combat carry more credibility with the VA than statements about non-combat events. Generally, if a combat veteran states that he or she suffered an injury during combat, the VA must accept this statement as fact. This makes sense. Those of us who have been there know all about the fog of war and the futility of trying to document all injuries during combat operations.

While a battalion may do a good job of capturing historical data on every IED blast that occurred in its area of operation, a list of soldiers affected by those IEDs is seldom available. Injuries incurred by OIF and OEF veterans from IED explosions, kicking in doors, and clearing rooms were fairly frequent but seldom reported.

Combat veterans also have a lower evidentiary burden to establish service connection for PTSD. If a veteran's stressor is related to combat, absent clear and convincing evidence to the contrary, the veteran's statement alone may establish the in-service stressor required for service connection for PTSD.

Requirement #3: Establishing a Nexus

Even if the VA acknowledges a current disability and an in-service injury or stressor, if a veteran cannot establish a link (or nexus) between the two, the VA will deny his or her claim.

A nexus is most commonly established with direct evidence of an in-service injury or aggravation of an existing disability. The nexus can be proven though military records coupled with recent VA or private physician examinations. The combination of service records and physician statements often naturally provides a link between the in-service event or injury and the current diagnosis.

Other times, a service-connected disability will cause an additional secondary disability. For example, a veteran with direct service connection for an injured right knee may later receive secondary service-connection for his or her right hip, as knee injuries often put stress on other areas of the lower body. When a veteran requests secondary service connection, he or she must demonstrate a connection between the direct service-connected disability and the secondary disability.

Non-medical professionals do not have the expertise to connect symptoms to a specific medical cause. Often, a veteran will meet the nexus requirement by submitting a letter from a VA physician or private physician that connects the veteran's disability to an in-service injury. The doctor will base his opinion on the veteran's C-File and other evidence.

The best medical nexus opinions list the information or evidence used by the doctor to form an opinion. The opinion might be based on medical records, a physical examination, the veteran's statements, or buddy statements. When the veteran's personal doctor provides a medical opinion, he or she can describe history of treatment, which may go a long way towards establishing a timeline that explains why the veteran's current disability was caused by an in-service injury.

Presumptive Service Connections

The VA presumes service connection for chronic diseases that become manifest to a degree of 10 percent or more within one year of separation from active service. Presumptive service connection also applies to diseases and disabilities connected to a veteran's exposure to a particular environment. Veterans who served in Southwest Asia after August 1990 are entitled to presumed service connection for undiagnosed illnesses commonly known as Gulf War Syndrome. Similarly, veterans who served in Vietnam or along the DMZ during certain time periods are presumed to have been exposed to Agent Orange.

Unfortunately, the presumption does not always result in service connection. The VA may take the position that a veteran who served in Vietnam diagnosed with a presumptive condition such as non-Hodgkin's Lymphoma should be denied service-connection. While it is presumptive that the veteran incurred the disease because of exposure to Agent Orange, if the VA has evidence to rebut that presumption, service connection will not be automatic.

While the presumption makes it easier for a veteran to obtain service connection for a disability, a veteran may still achieve direct service connection without the presumption. If the VA denies that a veteran has a right to the presumption, the veteran may still achieve service connection on a direct basis if he or she can establish a current diagnosis and a link between the disease or disability and military service.

Take Sam, who served in the Navy during the Vietnam War as a SeaBee (a member of the United States Naval Construction Forces). Due to Agent Orange exposure, Sam suffers from chlorachne, a condition that causes skin to erupt in cysts and pustules. The VA should have granted Sam presumptive service connection because cholorachne is one of the recognized diseases caused by Agent Orange exposure. However, the VA denied that Sam served in Vietnam and denied his claim. Sam eventually won his appeal thanks to before-and-after photographs and lay statements about the deterioration of his skin immediately after his discharge from the Navy.

After Action Review

There are multiple ways to achieve service connection. The key is meeting the three requirements explained in this chapter. A veteran must have (1) a current disability, disease, or illness (2) that was incurred during military service and (3) a medical link between an in-service injury or stressor and the current disability.

The most successful veterans don't rely on the VA to do the work or connect the dots. The most successful veterans take the initiative to get their own medical opinions and buddy statements and provide the VA with the documentation necessary to prove their current disability resulted from military service.

Chapter Two
Obtaining Correct Disability Ratings

After a veteran obtains service connection for a disability, the next fight is getting the correct disability rating. Veterans often feel cheated when the VA grants service connection at a minimal disability rating well below the veteran's degree of disability.

A disability rating is supposed to reflect the veteran's decreased ability to earn a living based on the severity of a service-connected disability. A higher rating means greater compensation. Veterans must remain vigilant after service connection to ensure they receive full compensation based on the correct disability rating.

VA disability ratings are generally increased in one of two situations:

1. A veteran receives an inadequate rating from the VA and appeals the VA Rating Decision.

2. A veteran requests an increase in compensation after his or her disability becomes worse over time.

Negating an Inadequate Rating

Allen, a Marine, was clearing a building in western Iraq when the floor collapsed, sending him 20 feet down onto a table in the room below. In the months after, Allen realized his back would never be the same.

Upon discharge, Allen filed a VA claim for his back condition. Six months later, the VA generated a rating decision awarding Allen a 10 percent disability rating. Understandably, Allen felt the VA failed to recognize the severity of his disability even though he thoroughly explained his condition to his VA doctor.

While looking over his rating decision, Allen found that the VA ignored many factors it should have considered according to the Code of Federal Regulations (CFR), so he filed an appeal known as a Notice of Disagreement (NOD) asking for an increased rating of at least 50 percent.

Eighteen months later, Allen received a decision from the VA granting his appeal and increasing his disability rating from 10 percent to 50 percent. The effective date of the new rating went all the way back to the date when he originally filed the claim, more than two years prior. Allen received a retroactive payment award of almost $20,000. Allen's monthly disability amount increased from approximately $130 a month to over $800 per month.

Requesting an Increased Disability Rating

Common sense and crusty first sergeants tell us that injuries either heal or get worse. Injuries that don't completely heal become disabilities which usually get worse over time. Veterans have the right to file for increased compensation as their disabilities worsen.

Amy, who served as a medic, injured a knee while trying to evacuate another solider when their convoy was attacked in Afghanistan. Amy's knee bothered her for over a year but by the time she was discharged it had mostly healed.
The VA service-connected her knee at zero percent. This means the VA acknowledged Amy had a service-connected disability but the disability was not severe enough to warrant compensation.

Two years later, Amy's symptoms worsened. Her pain increased and she lost range of motion in her knee. Amy requested that the VA increase her disability rating. Amy received a disability rating of 20 percent for her knee. Amy received a back pay award for the 8 months it took the VA to process her claim.

Inadequate Examinations Affect Disability Ratings

A common reason for improper ratings is inadequate VA examinations. A rating examination must contain both a description of the veteran's symptoms and the effects of the disability on the veteran's ordinary activities. The exam must also consider medical history. VA medical opinions must be based on facts from the veteran's records and past examinations.

When the VA fails to meet these standards, veterans are entitled to another examination. The VA rarely admits an examination was sub-standard, but the VA is required to provide another exam if a veteran successfully appeals the adequacy of the examination.

Occasionally, when a veteran has multiple disabilities, a VA doctor will assert that symptoms which should result in an increased rating come from a different non-service-connected disability. In these cases the VA will deny an increase in compensation. Veterans who appeal this issue frequently win because in many instances the veteran doesn't even have a diagnosis for the other "disability" the VA uses as a reason to deny the increase.

Mind your DBQs

Disability Benefits Questionnaires (or DBQs) are supposed to standardize the collection of medical evidence for processing VA claims. In theory, DBQs also ensure that private non-VA medical examinations comply with VA standards for purposes of determining disability ratings.

Successful veterans consider the DBQ the minimal standard and provide the VA with additional information not covered in the DBQ when appealing their VA claims. A private doctor who completes the DBQ on behalf of a veteran needs to be aware that he or she is not limited to checking the boxes presented on the VA form and may attach a narrative to the DBQ to better explain the severity of a veteran's disability. DBQs are like most checklist systems: They provide uniformity, which can improve accuracy. Problems arise when the DBQs contradict the VA's C&P examination.

The Wrong Diagnostic Code

Once the VA determines a veteran's disability is service-connected, the VA looks in the Code of Federal Regulations for the appropriate disability diagnostic code and chooses the disability rating percentage. Occasionally the VA applies an incorrect diagnostic code. This happens when the VA ignores favorable rating criteria or imposes additional criteria not listed in the diagnostic code.

Problems occur when a single disability may be rated under more than one diagnostic code. In these instances, the VA is required to choose the code that yields the highest disability percentage. When the VA fails to do so, a veteran may appeal the decision, asking to be rated under the diagnostic code that would give the highest possible rating.

Close Only Counts in Hand Grenades and Higher Ratings

When analyzing a VA Rating Decision, a veteran will find that he or she fits some but not all of the criteria listed for a higher rating. When there is a question as to whether a veteran's disability better fits a higher or lower rating, the VA is required to assign the higher one. In other words, if a veteran has a disability that supports both a 30 percent and a 50 percent rating, the VA should rate the veteran at the higher percentage of 50 percent. The VA often incorrectly requires evidence of all listed rating criteria in order to assign a specific rating level. If a veteran's disability more closely resembles the higher rating, the veteran gets the higher rating regardless of whether a veteran suffers from all of the symptoms listed in the higher rating criteria.

Sloppy Staged Ratings

The VA may assign separate ratings for different time periods if a veteran's condition changes between the date he or she filed a claim and the date the appeal was assigned.

For example, Judy filed a claim in 2010 for PTSD stemming from military sexual trauma (MST). The VA provided Judy with a C&P examination but denied her claim. Judy filed a Notice of Disagreement appealing the decision. The VA regional office again denied her claim, so Judy appealed her case to the BVA. In 2012, while her case was on appeal, Judy received another medical examination which noted additional mental health symptoms. By the time the BVA granted Judy service connection for PTSD in 2014, her condition had significantly worsened.

The BVA granted Judy service connection for PTSD with a 30 percent disability rating from the time she initially filed her claim in 2010 until the VA received new evidence of increased disability in 2012. From 2012 onwards, Judy was granted service connection for PTSD at 50 percent. Judy again appealed the VA's decision arguing she should have been rated at 70 percent and that the worsening of her condition was already present but had not been noted in the 2012 examination.

In 2016, after the case was remanded by the CAVC, the VA determined that Judy should receive a 50 percent rating all the way back to 2010 and that her ratings should not have been staged. Judy did not get service connected at 70 percent, but she received a significant back pay award when the VA determined her initial disability rating should be 50 percent rather than 30 percent between the years of 2010 and 2012.

Accurately Rating Mental Disabilities

When the VA rates mental disabilities (like PTSD), it focuses on occupational and social impairment. Occupational impairment measures how much a disability affects a veteran's ability to work. Social impairment measures the veteran's ability to establish and maintain relationships with others. In some instances, the social and occupational impairments can affect each other. For example, a veteran uncomfortable in crowded spaces or unable to develop relationships may find that these social symptoms affect his or her ability to perform in a work environment that requires interaction with others.

The frequency and severity of symptoms are also important in evaluating the disability rating. The VA must consider the entire history of the mental disability. Buddy statements are a great way to establish frequency and severity of a veteran's symptoms over time. Family members, close friends, and spouses can help the VA understand symptoms displayed on a veteran's "bad days," and the extent to which the disability affects the veteran's ability to perform as an employee, spouse, or parent.

David, an infantry soldier who earned the Combat Infantryman Badge in Vietnam, was honorably discharged in 1973. When David went to the VA for mental health conditions associated with his service, the VA brushed him aside and never adjudicated his claim (this was before PTSD was a recognized mental disability). In 1998, David again applied for disability for his mental health condition and the VA awarded him a 70 percent rating for PTSD. The VA determined the effective date of the claim to be the day David refiled the claim in 1998. David disagreed with the effective date and requested that the VA grant an effective date all the way back to 1973, the date he initially filed his claim with the VA. After a long period of appeals that went all the way up to the CAVC, the VA eventually granted David the 1973 effective date.

Unfortunately, instead of awarding David the 70 percent rating he received in 1998, the VA awarded David a 10 percent rating from 1973 to 1998. David prepared to fight the rating because his PTSD symptoms had not changed since 1973 and the VA provided no valid basis for the initial 10 percent rating. He again appealed the decision and two years later received a 70 percent rating going all the way back to 1973.

Although David eventually obtained the compensation he deserved, the process infuriated him. The VA provided no logical reason as to why he was initially awarded only 10 percent from 1973 to 1998. This contradicted David's medical records which showed he had displayed the same symptoms since 1973.

David's story is an all-too-common example of a veteran who had to fight to get service connected, fight to acquire the correct disability rating, and fight to receive the appropriate back pay award.

After Action Review

Veterans who want to fix their low rating problem often want to "fix bayonets" and charge forward with appeals. However, obtaining the correct rating will take time and effort, even in the most obvious situations.

Chapter Three
Real Effective Dates

Once the VA grants service connection and sets a disability rating, it must determine the correct effective date. This is important because the effective date determines when the VA begins to owe the veteran disability compensation.

Because it takes the VA a long time to decide claims and appeals, most service-connected veterans receive retroactive payments (known as back pay awards). These payments can be substantial when a disabled veteran files a claim, waits months for a VA decision, and then waits years for the VA to decide the appeal.

For example, if a veteran filed a claim for PTSD on December 1, 2014 and the VA issued a rating decision on August 1, 2015 granting service connection with a 50 percent rating, the veteran would be entitled to eight months of back pay. This means that starting August 1, 2015 the veteran would receive monthly compensation of $917.13 (based on the 2014 compensation rate) and a lump sum back pay award of $7,337,04. The back pay award covers the time from the date the veteran filed the claim to the time the VA decided the claim in the veteran's favor.

Now consider the more common result: Twelve months after a veteran initially files a claim, the VA denies it. The veteran then files an appeal which takes an additional 24 months to process. Assuming the veteran was entitled to compensation at the time the claim was filed, he or she is now entitled to receive 36 months of back pay (more than $33,000).

The general rule for effective dates of original claims is that the clock starts the day the VA receives the claim or the date that the veteran became entitled to the benefit, whichever is later. When a veteran files a claim within one year from the date of discharge from active duty, the veteran's effective date will be the day after his or her discharge. However, if a veteran fails to appeal a VA decision and later refiles a claim, the effective date is usually the date of the refiled claim.

The High Price of Failing to Appeal

Sadly, many veterans whose claims are denied become discouraged and decide not to appeal. Later, when these veterans decide to fight for their benefits, they discover they've lost years of compensation. Once they refile their claims, the effective date will be the day the VA receives the request to reopen the claim. This means the veteran loses the original effective date.

Alex, for example, filed a claim for disability benefits when she was discharged from the Air Force in 2010. Alex was in college when the VA denied her claim, and felt that she did not have time to appeal. In the absence of an appeal, her rating decision became final. Four years later, when Alex tried to reopen her claim, she learned that the effective date of her disability payments would be September 2014, not 2010.

If Alex had successfully appealed within one year of receiving her rating decision, she would have received compensation with a back pay award going back to August 2010.

Alex's failure to appeal cost her four years, or thousands of dollars, of potential back pay. And that's not all: The VA refused to grant Alex's refiled claim because she did not have the "new and material evidence" required to reopen it. Once a VA decision becomes final, the veteran may not reopen the claim by submitting the same evidence.

The bottom line: If a veteran fails to appeal a claim there are road blocks that will make it more difficult for the veteran to get service-connected for that claim in the future.

CUE - The Effective Date Rescue

Veterans and attorneys regularly find cases in which the VA made an obvious error in denying a claim. This is called Clear and Unmistakable Error (or CUE). In this instance, the effective date goes back to that of the original claim.

While CUE may get a veteran an earlier effective date, it does not mean he or she will be retrospectively rated at the same level as his or her current disability rating. The VA must determine what the disability rating would have been if the veteran had been properly granted service connection. As we learned from David's story (in which he had to fight the VA multiple times to get the benefits he deserved), getting the correct disability rating is an entirely different fight.

When the VA Fails to Issue a Decision

Sometimes the VA will lose a claim or neglect to adjudicate it. In these cases, a veteran is entitled to the effective date of his or her original claim.

For example, if a Vietnam veteran files a claim in 1972 and the VA fails to issue a rating decision, this claim is still pending today. When the same veteran files a claim for the same disability and receives compensation, the effective date may go all the way back to 1972.

Blaming the Veteran

Veterans have not always submitted VA claim forms when requesting disability compensation. The law previously allowed veterans to make "informal claims" for disability benefits. Over the years, veterans and the VA have fought over what exactly constitutes an informal claim. Sometimes the VA uses the wording of a veteran's informal claim to argue the claim was not reasonably raised instead of just admitting that they failed to process it.

The VA may also argue that they informally denied a claim - without explicitly telling the veteran about it. This is known as the Implicit Denial Rule. Despite the obvious due process violations, the VA regularly makes this argument to deny veterans earlier effective dates.

Effective Dates for Informal Claims

Prior to March 24, 2015, a claim was defined as a formal or informal written communication requesting VA compensation. Thus, any action indicating intent to obtain VA benefits qualified as a claim regardless of whether or not a veteran filled out a form. When the VA failed to process these informal claims, veterans were entitled to the effective dates of their initial informal claims.

Effective March 24, 2015, a veteran must formally file a claim using a VA form. If a veteran fails to submit this form in a timely manner, it could alter his or her effective date. A lawsuit challenging the elimination of the informal claim is currently pending.

Despite this new formal claim requirement, veterans continue to argue that the VA failed in its obligation to adjudicate their informal claims.

Effective Dates for TDIU Claims

TDIU stands for Total Disability Based on Individual Unemployability. Veterans who have a disability rating of less than 100 percent but cannot maintain gainful employment due to their disabilities may qualify for TDIU.

The VA often incorrectly assesses TDIU effective dates. Failing to attain the correct effective date for TDIU claims can cost veterans an enormous amount of disability compensation.

A veteran may request unemployability compensation by submitting VA Form 21-8940 to his or her regional office. In some circumstances, the VA must consider a veteran's entitlement to TDIU even if a form is never submitted. This is because the correct effective date for a TDIU claim is the day the VA becomes aware of a veteran's inability to work, regardless of whether the veteran submitted a form.

Sometimes, the VA receives evidence of a veteran's unemployability when he or she files a claim for service connection and indicates that symptoms are preventing him or her from maintaining employment. If the VA grants service connection, a veteran's entitlement to receive TDIU must be considered, even if he or she did not formally request TDIU benefits.

If a veteran provides evidence of his or her unemployability after the VA grants service connection for a disability, the VA must consider whether TDIU is appropriate. In these cases, the effective date would either be the day the VA received the claim for service connection or the day the veteran became unemployable, whichever is later.

Finally, if a veteran requests an increased disability rating and provides the VA with evidence of unemployability, the effective date is either the date the VA received the claim for an increased rating or the date the veteran became unemployable because of his service-connected disability, whichever is later.

Capturing the Earliest Effective Date

When the VA determines the effective date for benefits, it must consider when the veteran became entitled to compensation. In most cases, veterans who wait to obtain supporting evidence before filing a claim regret not filing earlier. As far as effective dates go, a claim filed now without substantiating documentation is better than a well-documented claim filed six months later. Once a veteran files a claim, the VA will provide time for him or her to offer evidence or undergo a C&P examination. By taking the time to collect evidence before filing, veterans can miss out on several months, if not years, of disability compensation.

Filing a claim as quickly as possible is especially important in PTSD cases. Veterans who suffer from psychological problems often don't obtain a diagnosis upon discharge; they usually wait until their symptoms become more severe before seeking medical attention. If a veteran obtains a medical opinion indicating he or she suffered from symptoms associated with PTSD prior to a formal diagnosis, then he or she can argue that entitlement to service connection arose once those symptoms originally manifested. There is nothing wrong with submitting claims for PTSD prior to obtaining a diagnosis.

Take Seth for example, who submitted a claim for PTSD in 2009. At the time, he had recently been discharged from the Marine Corps and had not been diagnosed with PTSD. His regional office denied his claim 12 months later. Seth appealed by filing a Notice of Disagreement and attaching buddy statements corroborating his PTSD symptoms. While his appeal was pending, Seth obtained a diagnosis for PTSD and the VA service-connected him.

Unfortunately, because the VA determined Seth didn't meet all the criteria for PTSD service connection on the date the VA received his claim, the VA set his effective date 18 months later, the date he was diagnosed with PTSD. Seth appealed this decision, arguing that his PTSD symptoms manifested long before he obtained a medical opinion. Seth also re-submitted buddy statements in support of his appeal.

In most cases, it is to a veteran's benefit to submit a claim as early as possible. Even though Seth was not diagnosed with PTSD when he filed his claim, his decision to move ahead with his claim won him a substantial back pay award years later.

The VA's Duty to Assist

The VA exists to provide veterans with medical treatment and assistance when obtaining the benefits they earn through their service to our country. The VA's role at the agency level is "non-adversarial." This means it has a duty to help qualified veterans through the claims process.

When the VA fails to assist a veteran seeking benefits, the veteran may claim that he or she made an informal claim and therefore is entitled to an earlier effective date based on the VA's failure to assist. Even if the odds of success are low, a veteran has the right to present an argument and hold the VA to the legal standard associated with its duty to assist.

After Action Review

The earlier a veteran files a claim with the VA, the earlier an effective date can be set. Veterans who appeal VA decisions quickly avoid losing their original effective dates, potentially saving thousands of dollars in compensation. Fortunately for veterans who neglected to appeal, if the VA is found to have made a clear and unmistakable error in denying a claim or fails to address a claim, lost effective dates may be restored.

Culmination

Obtaining VA benefits can be difficult. Many veterans have to fight to obtain service connection for their disabilities. Even service-connected veterans must continue to fight for correct disability ratings and effective dates.

A veteran can proactively pursue his or her claim by providing the VA with evidence in the form of independent medical opinions, buddy statements, photographs, service records and other documents.

The battle for veterans' disability benefits may seem futile at times. Veterans are rightfully frustrated with the time and effort it takes to obtain the benefits they've already earned. However, after many years representing thousands of veterans, I have never known a veteran to regret his or her pursuit of VA disability benefits.

For more about veterans' disability claims, please visit ptsdlawyers.com.

Are You Appealing a VA Disability Claim?

If you serve your country, it should stand behind you if you are injured in the line of duty. The Berry Law Firm is committed to securing the benefits you need and deserve through all levels of appeals. To speak with a member of our team, please call **888.883.2483** or visit us online at **ptsdlawyers.com**. Your consultation is free. We take VA cases on a contingency fee basis. If we accept your case, you will pay no fee to us unless we recover benefits for you.

Please share this book with other veterans struggling with the appeals process. Send a request to **book@ptsdlawyers.com** for a free copy. Supplies are limited, so contact us today.

Acronyms

BVA .... Board of Veterans Appeals
C-File .... Claims File
C&P .... Compensation and Pension
CAVC .... Court of Appeals for Veterans Claims
CFR .... Code of Federal Regulations
CUE .... Clear and Unmistakable Error
DBQ .... Disability Benefits Questionnaires
DMZ .... Demilitarized Zone
IDT .... Inactive-Duty Training
IED .... Improvised Explosive Device
IME .... Independent Medical Examination
MST .... Military Sexual Trauma
NOD .... Notice of Disagreement
OEF .... Operation Enduring Freedom
OIF .... Operation Iraqi Freedom
PTSD .... Post-Traumatic Stress Disorder
RO .... Regional Office
TDIU Total Disability Based on Individual Unemployability
VA .... Department of Veterans Affairs
VAMC .... Veterans Administration Medical Center
VARO .... Veterans Affairs Regional Office

Index

Notes on Your VA Disability Claim

Made in the USA
Middletown, DE
30 September 2019